her soul was too deep
to explore by those who
always swam in the shallow end.

A Little Poetic

Teresa James

Dedicated To:

Everyone who reads and
has shown interest in my poetry.
Much love and blessings to you all.

Preface

Listen to the space between the words
and you can hear the cry of the poet
who wrote a moving piece.

Listen to the pause break and you
can decipher the inner struggle.

Listen to the comma and the hyphen
and you will know the hardship we bestow.

Listen to the sound of the pen as we bleed
from within to tell a tale no one knows.

~

A short poem that moves you
is powerful.
A long poem that keeps you
is impressive.

Inner Beauty

I want to be beautiful
all of the time.

I will remain beautiful
if I'm not feeling fine.

I want to be beautiful
when the sky is gray.

I will remain beautiful,
come what may.

Why plant a flower if you're
not going to care for it?
Why water a rose if you're
not going to maintain it?
Why say you love me if you're
not going to prove it?

My instincts tell me you're
a player by the way you move.
But your eyes speak a
depth of honesty and trust.

My past tells me to wait
and see if you're trustworthy.
But my gut says—he's the one.

I'm patient…

I'll wait, in time your actions
may prove what I see in your eyes.
If not, your loss, not mine.

I will fight for love
but I will not
compete for it.

I forgave you but
didn't forget you.
I miss you but
can't reach you.
I am in pain but
maybe one day
I'll be less insane.
My confession is
love and you've
taught me a lesson.

In the distance
I heard your call.

My love for you
does stand tall.

Trust me & I will
give you my all.

We have each other
and we shall not fall.

What do I see when I look
into your eyes, my love?
Intriguing depths of
my own heart do I see.
Passion deeply within
ignites the fire in my skin,
and tantalizing on a whim.
Touching the very warmth
of you moves through me.
Loving you is meant to be,
while kissing you gently.
I see me...

Whispers of the
darkness brings fear.

Wishing for light to
bring comfort near.

Wandering thoughts
seem to go far away.

Wishing for peaceful
moments in the day.

Whispers of the soft
light brings stability.

Wandering thoughts
leads to tranquility.

Secrets and lies
beneath the lines.
Truth disguised as
the darkness blinds.
Who knows where
raging winds blow.
In my mind is where
delusions seem to go.
Haunting memories of
the past creeping in
like cancerous mass.
Remedies for a cure;
Can't take this anymore!

Afternoon Stroll

Take a walk with me,
and let's stop to lay
beneath the lovers
tree in the valley.
I will tell you my
dreams and maybe
even my fantasies.

Gazing into your eyes
is a delight indeed.
The aroma of the
flowers present in
the air leads me to
run my fingers
through your hair.

Oh my darling, you
are like the cherry
blossoms to me.
A sure sign, as the
first days of spring.
To give you my love
awaits a wedding ring.

My love, my heart beats for you and there is no other.
Rest assured—my treasures have been hidden for you to find.

My cup tips over with
fullness of passion for you.
Never will your thirst run dry;
my love is better than wine.
Sip with ease as I please
the desire of your taste.
Not one drip will ever
be a waste.

My Sanity

I love you, but
Having interaction
with you disrupts
my mental peace.

A Dead End.

I surely love you
but from afar.
Sorry Sir Toxic
but not sorry—
I sustain my peace.

The eyes, Do lie—
telling you what they see.
At times it's not even reality.
Whispering to your mind to paint
a picture of what's not there.

Is it deceit you smell in the atmosphere
or the mere delusion of your fear?
Distorted senses, causes false pretenses.
So you walk in darkness during the day.

Reach out and let your soul touch reality.
Never pretend, don't be a slave to agony.
Let your heart whisper to your eyes;
I don't believe you, Do Not Lie…

Yearning in the velvet skies.
Drying the tears from my eyes.
Wishing for a different feeling.

Escaping the downtrodden blue.
Searching in the darkness for...
Another version, a deeper hue.

Hoping for my lover to reveal.
All the madness he had me feel.
Time is a deceiver to be healed.

I am honest and integrity is real.
Purple moonlight, soft as can be.
Speak to my soul, let me be free.

In darkness you are my light and my shadow in the day.
You're my comfort in the storm—lips who keep me warm.

As a flicker turns to flame;
my love is your sun after the rain.

Depression

The sky is grey today and
the sounds I hear bring fear.
The darkness grips me tight
while holding me near and dear.

My days are long, nights are cold.
These feelings never become old.
Just a lingering sense of wasted time;
which keeps ticking inside my mind.

Always wondering if hope is blind.
Will the sun shine on me one day?
I remain thinking the sky is grey...

*SILENCE
SPEAKS...*

Buttercup

There's so much joy and
nostalgia in the simple
things in life.

Like...
I stopped to pick
buttercups while taking
a morning stroll.

What a delight;
it's like they were
dancing brightly
under the sunlight.

Her beauty is
delicate as a daisy and
stands out like a rose.
She is subtle as a cool
summer breeze and
captivating like
the wind.

Love paved the pathway
as you came into my life.

Our love became solidified
when I received your child,
embracing him inside of me.

Our lifestyles will change and
days will never be the same;
a joy to give our son a name.

Our union was my destiny and
I warmly honor my pregnancy.
Love has manifested within.

It started off as
You and Me.
Our Love turned
into Three.

You're the groundskeeper of my heart.
Who tends to my earthly needs for growth.
When the wind blows—I sway your way.
You smell the aroma of jasmine and caraway.
Feel the softness of the petals in the palm
of your hand, then I whisper in your ear...
"Come water your garden" as you draw near.
Lover of my soul and the only one I hold dear.

If I had a penny for
every second
I think of you.
Then I would count
every minute
my heart skips a beat
in your presence.

I want to kiss you
forever and hold you
in my arms for eternity.

My love for you has no
bounds and the depths
go beyond the seas.

We're made for each other…

You've taught me pure
ecstasy and proved to me
how a true love should be.

Wishes *do* come true and
I've surely found mine in you.

Sorry

Sorry is for when you
step on someone's toe.
Sorry is for the mistake
and you just didn't know.
Sorry is for little things
that weren't meant to happen.
Sorry is not for when you've
broken someone's heart.
Sorry just doesn't heal the parts...

The time passed so fast...
Without realizing you weren't
building a love with me to last.
Everything I needed from you,
wasn't in your character to do.

I saw the red flags,
and yet still I kept trying...
While in my heart I was crying;
hoping you would trust and
become stronger in your faith.

Perfect love is not always fate.
Honey, it may be a little too late.
Application of honesty is a must.
It's the only way to build solid trust.
Loving you has been stressful too.

Nonetheless I have given the best.
Because my love is pure, you I adore.
Your insecurities I could have mend.
If you didn't pretend and had let me in.
Although it was my heart, you did win.

I started to write you a poem but
couldn't find the right words to say.
To express how I'm feeling inside;
hoping to get the words out this time.
Maybe a gentle kiss on the lips will do?
So you can feel what I want to say—
I desire you and my love is true.

Wherever you are,
is where I want to be.

Under the moonlight holding you
tight is where I always want to be.

~

Where the stars shine pleasantly.
Where my heart meets its destiny.
Where the music plays magically.
Where you kiss me romantically.

Wandering through the dark
is where I've always been.
I didn't know there was light
and didn't have true friends.

Just a lonely girl,
with no sense of direction.
I wondered why I never fit in
and so very different within.

I never saw a reflection of myself
until one day I heard from God.
He said, draw near to me and
tell me what you see?

As I got closer I replied, "I see Me".

And from that day on...
I no longer looked for the light.
Because I was the light;
I could not see.

Never dim your
light because it
shines too bright
for someone
else's eyes.

If he's a player—
think twice.
He'll toss your
feelings like dice.
Leave you broken
in the end.
He won't be seen
like the wind.

The Narcissist

You want what you don't give.
You take what you don't have.
You use and abuse me to live.
Like a drug you need your fix.
Twisting words is your game.
You pretend just to gain fame.
You leave your victims broken.
Words of manipulation spoken.
Unethical healer is what you do.
Karma will come back on you.

He says he loves me
Yet I bleed from his cuts
Words are fatal and rough
Torn and humiliated enough
Then he wants to patch me up
Back on the rollercoaster again
While my heart is bleeding within
Seeing nothing wrong in his ways
While always begging me to stay
Until tomorrow when I bleed again

At times, the best thing you can
do for yourself is to be alone.
Meditate on you, and go to a
special place in your mind.
Relax and find peace in
just knowing yourself.

Up and down
In and out
Round about
Make you shout
Truly no doubt
I'll stay on top
Til you say stop
Make me pop
You keep me hot
Take me there
Pull my hair
I'll kiss you too
Til you're through
Rest and relax
Come back
Take it to the max
I'm all for you
You love me too
Passion stays new
Never out of tune
I'll always want you

Let me touch you in the place
where no one has been before.
I will search the depths of your soul
and find the sensuous in you.
I will delight your mind and lead
you to a place only we can find.

A day with me won't
always be rosey or daisy;
sometimes you will see the thorns.

A day with me won't
always be sunny rays;
sometimes you will see the storms.

I love you with every
fiber of my being—

I realize we're not cut
from the same cloth.

But we'll come together
as patchwork sewn tight.

My faithful lover in the
day and through the night.

You bring me comfort, so
I will be your comforter too.

If dreams were reality and
every fantasy came true.
I would spend my time
in a fairytale with you.
Where you can always be
my knight and shining armor,
I'll be your princess too.
Making love on a rainbow
in ecstasy with you.

Take me on a
secret rendezvous to
where my imagination roams.
Where time stops and
fantasy is our zone.

Run and hide from your treacherous lies
while I bleed from torn emotional ties.
But it was like laying naked in the rain.
As I basked in the brutal pain.

I just want to forget and erase your name.
You cut me and I bled for hours long.
For you to perform a surgery that would
end the rapid raging flow of blood;
with a simple touch of a word.

Appease me by acknowledging
the ways you have hurt me.
I am still healing from the onslaught.
Although will assuredly recover
little-by-little, as if I was unscathed.

The love of my life
whom I truly adore—
I never fathomed not to
want your love anymore.
You pushed me away
while begging me to stay.
I will heal and move on;
come what may.

It feels like without you, my life
is incomplete and I can't go on.

I put a smile on my face every day,
pretending to be ok but I am torn.

Many nights I cry myself to sleep
wondering if my pain will ever cease.

My love for you runs deep,
like the depths of the oceans floor.

My heartache is the reality that you
are no longer in my life anymore.

If I could turn back the hands of the
clock to when you became out of line.

Maybe you could dry my weeping
eyes and treat me better this time.

Purple is my passion and the
symbol of royalty, although love
upholds my precious loyalty.

Many men seek the tranquility
of what rests in the soul of
mother nature's fertility.

Wisdom and honor are my backbone;
Grace and mercy are the embodiment
of the secrets I behold.

Time has never been my friend;
Yet eternal life is offered in the end.
My love is held deep inside.

With healing power, to cover sin.
Broken hearts I want to mend;
Let the restoration truly begin.

Surely you could drown
in the depths of my heart.
If the waves haven't
already kept us apart.
Dont tread the waters
learn how to stay afloat.
The current is strong &
my love is your lifeboat.

My love is deeper than
the depths of the seas.
Lover, be careful with me,
understand how deep it is.
For you will drown,
if you don't swim.

I'm writing you this letter
hoping it will make
my heart feel better.
The words are bottled
up inside, as I write
I begin to cry.
If only you would
communicate and try.
It wouldn't feel like
the well has run dry;
in this shit you
call a relationship.
I wouldn't be sitting
here writing on paper
while my tears drip.

Captured by your smile—delighted with your kiss.
Your love is the comfort deep within my spirit.

Every minute I spend in your
presence is my pleasure.
I am always satisfied—a mere kiss
from you tastes like honeydew.

I want to go to a place unknown.
Where there's no sadness
and the air smells like home.
Where peace is the comfort zone
and tame majestic beast roam.
Where the grass is always green
and the people are never mean.
Where the birds chirp their songs
and children play all day long.
Where joy rises in the east
and sets peacefully in the west.
In this place my soul rests.

God, there's no need
to be seen when your words
can move mountains.

When birds sing their happy songs
from the presence of your love.
When the flowers in the
meadows sway all day.

When the warm days bring
a sweet gentle breeze.
When the moon appears
at nightfall with ease.

When the lilies of the valley
bloom so graciously.
There's no need to be seen
when you are all the goodness
in the earth to see.

kiss me quick and make me weak
take my power, my voice to speak
lead me into the pouring rain
love me like you'll never love again

THEN

break my heart and cause me tears
leave me scars to heal within years
try not to mend my broken soul and
leave me to become whole for
you to build and break me again

THEN

want to be the everlasting shoulder
for tears eternity your smothering eyes
won't be able to crawl for it was
one cut too many, to heal at all

I'll look to the sky with open
arms and embrace my worth.
Love prevails and blossoms;
I am the salt of the earth.

Truth can set you free and
even lead you to eternity.

Deep inside we all believe
to know what we perceive.

In the darkness we see lies
and hate is in the sky.

The air we breathe bleeds
for what the Earth needs.

Truth is the light and we all
have a plight—at the end
of the tunnel of life.

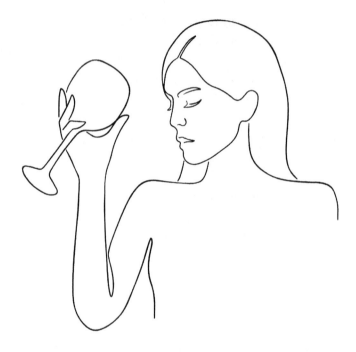

I want to run, I want to hide
From all the pain he caused inside.
I want to scream, I want to cry.
Why can't I tell him goodbye?

I want to move on; I just can't let go.
I love him more than he will ever know.
I want to start over, I want to feel free!
But this pain will never leave me be.

He hurt me bad; the pain is deep.
From all the promises he couldn't keep.
All the lies I heard him say...
Are in my head and just won't fade.

How can I forget him, leave him behind?
Erase the memories from my mind?
He doesn't love me, and he never will.
He will never care how truly I feel.

I need a place in my mind to unwind.
So I sip my wine and pass the time.
But the memories of him still linger...
That he let me slip through his fingers.

Kiss me like
there's no tomorrow.

Even if there was
some time to borrow.

My heart will never
feel any sorrow.

With your love I will
hope for tomorrow.

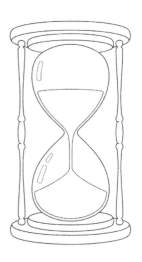

Waiting on true love is…

Waiting for the special
one who respects love
as much as you do.

Who wants love to work
as much as you do.

Who wants to give love
as much as you do.

Waiting on true love is…

Respecting love enough
to know when you've
encountered the one.

Who truly values love
as much as you do.

I am a beautiful flower garden
my blossoms must be cared for.
To search for a groundskeeper;
I should chose someone who can
properly maintain and cultivate.

I found him and he loves flowers
and sees the beauty in my garden.
I was impressed with the bountiful love
which he has for the aroma & essence.

Soon I began to see his maintenance
through my own rose colored glasses.
He adores my garden although he lacked
the ability of handling a botanical majesty.

My garden began to suffer and I couldn't
see clearly that my roses were dying.
Countless weeds were beginning to
choke all my precious beautiful flowers.
His damage to me was insidious...

I hired the wrong groundskeeper
based on his desire & love of flowers.
Not considering that he had no knowledge
and understanding on how to tend
to such a precious garden.

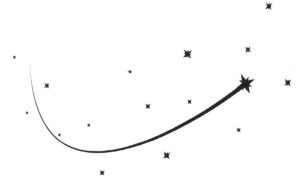

If your dream is to
find a star, stop looking
towards the ground.

I am the kind of poem which
many cannot quite understand.
My words puncture the soul
and cut through hard layers
of the disbelief one beholds.

I'll tell you deep hidden truths
that have never been told.
Mysteries of the divine which
have been covered through time.

To be released into the heart
of the one who relates to mine.
Peace and tranquility is the end;
only if honesty is your best friend.

Because she competes with no one,
No one can compete with her.

About Author

Teresa James is known for her poetry and art
shared throughout social media as Love of a Poet.
Where you can actually interact with her. She is passionate about
the creativity and beauty of poetry. She mostly writes short poems
about love and relationships. She is a mother of seven children,
a horticulturist, and philanthropist. While going through heartbreaks,
struggles, and grief throughout life. She learned to write her emotions
down on paper to vent and release pain. She now bleeds ink by writing
and sharing through her poetry.

www.TeresaJamesPoetry.com

Made in the USA
Middletown, DE
13 June 2021

42142715R00050